THE GREAT AMERICAN SONGBOOK

15 TIMELESS CLASSICS ARRANGED BY PHILLIP KEVEREN

— PIANO LEVEL —
LATE INTERMEDIATE/EARLY ADVANCED

ISBN 978-1-4950-7099-0

HAL•LEONARD® CORPORATION

7777 W. BLUEMOUND RD. P.O. BOX 13819 MILWAUKEE, WI 53213

Visit Hal Leonard Online at
www.halleonard.com

Visit Phillip at
www.phillipkeveren.com

PREFACE

The "standards" from the early 20th century are often referred to as The Great American Songbook. There is no official list of these evergreen songs, but there are hundreds, if not thousands – including songs composed for Broadway shows and films of this era.

I have whittled the list down to 15 of my favorites, and that was no easy task. With names like George Gershwin, Jerome Kern, Cole Porter, Irving Berlin, et al. adorning these gems, the sheer number of exquisite songs from which to choose is breathtaking.

I hope you enjoy these piano arrangements. It is a privilege to have the opportunity to present them.

Sincerely,

Phillip Keveren

BIOGRAPHY

Phillip Keveren, a multi-talented keyboard artist and composer, has composed original works in a variety of genres from piano solo to symphonic orchestra. Mr. Keveren gives frequent concerts and workshops for teachers and their students in the United States, Canada, Europe, and Asia. Mr. Keveren holds a B.M. in composition from California State University Northridge and a M.M. in composition from the University of Southern California.

CONTENTS

ALL THE THINGS YOU ARE

from VERY WARM FOR MAY

Lyrics by OSCAR HAMMERSTEIN II
Music by JEROME KERN
Arranged by Phillip Keveren

ALL THE WAY
from THE JOKER IS WILD

Words by SAMMY CAHN
Music by JAMES VAN HEUSEN
Arranged by Phillip Keveren

AUTUMN IN NEW YORK

Words and Music by
VERNON DUKE
Arranged by Phillip Keveren

BLUE SKIES

from BETSY

Words and Music by
IRVING BERLIN
Arranged by Phillip Keveren

COME RAIN OR COME SHINE

from ST. LOUIS WOMAN

Words by JOHNNY MERCER
Music by HAROLD ARLEN
Arranged by Phillip Keveren

Slowly, expressively (♩ = 76-80)

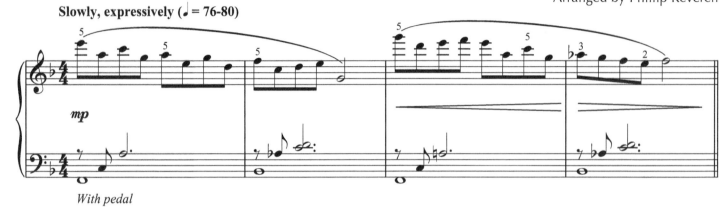

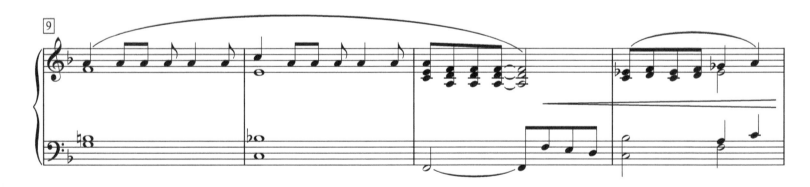

IF EVER I WOULD LEAVE YOU

from CAMELOT

Words by ALAN JAY LERNER
Music by FREDERICK LOEWE
Arranged by Phillip Keveren

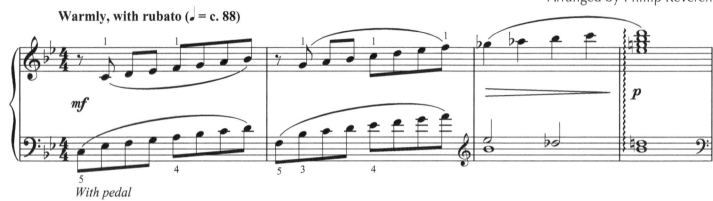

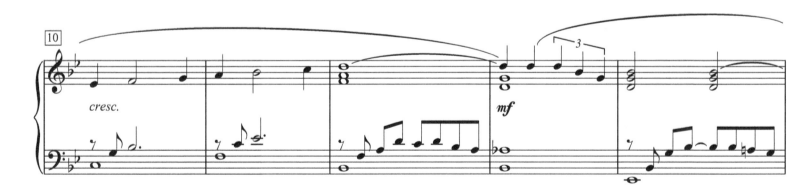

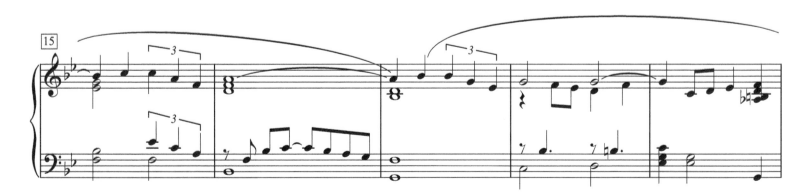

IN THE STILL OF THE NIGHT

from ROSALIE

Words and Music by
COLE PORTER
Arranged by Phillip Keveren

Flowing (♩ = 96)

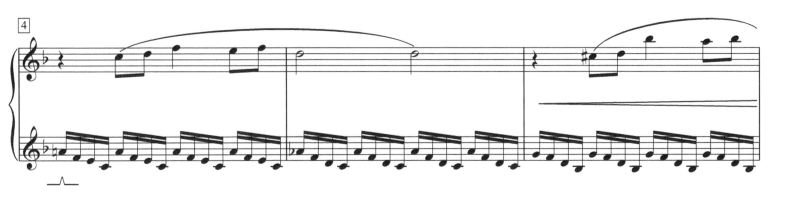

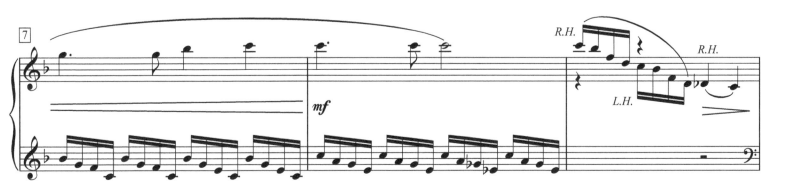

ISN'T IT ROMANTIC?
from the Paramount Picture LOVE ME TONIGHT

Words by LORENZ HART
Music by RICHARD RODGERS
Arranged by Phillip Keveren

MONA LISA
from the Paramount Picture CAPTAIN CAREY, U.S.A.

Words and Music by JAY LIVINGSTON
and RAY EVANS
Arranged by Phillip Keveren

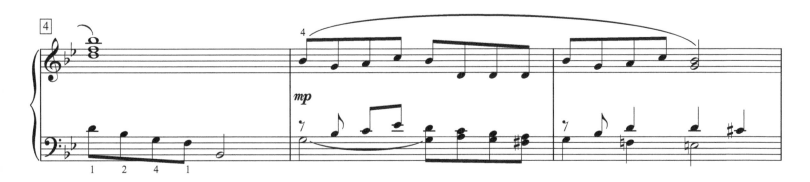

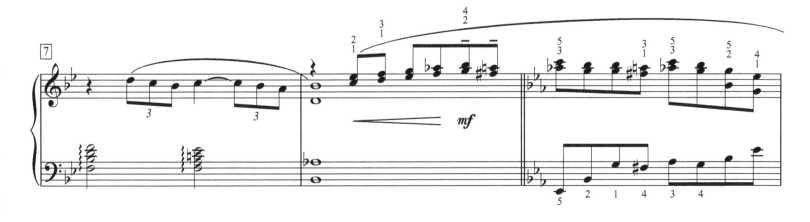

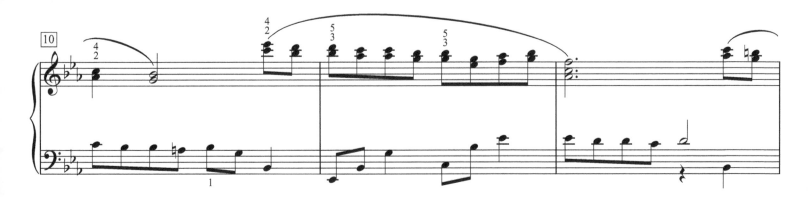

SKYLARK

Words by JOHNNY MERCER
Music by HOAGY CARMICHAEL
Arranged by Phillip Keveren

SUMMERTIME
from PORGY AND BESS®

Music and Lyrics by GEORGE GERSHWIN,
DuBOSE and DOROTHY HEYWARD and IRA GERSHWIN
Arranged by Phillip Keveren

THERE WILL NEVER BE ANOTHER YOU

from the Motion Picture ICELAND

Lyric by MACK GORDON
Music by HARRY WARREN
Arranged by Phillip Keveren

TIME AFTER TIME

from the Metro-Goldwyn-Mayer Picture IT HAPPENED IN BROOKLYN

Words by SAMMY CAHN
Music by JULE STYNE
Arranged by Phillip Keveren

WHEN YOU WISH UPON A STAR

Words by NED WASHINGTON
Music by LEIGH HARLINE

TAKE THE "A" TRAIN

Words and Music by
BILLY STRAYHORN
Arranged by Phillip Keveren

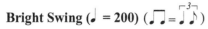

THE PHILLIP KEVEREN SERIES

PIANO SOLO

ABBA FOR CLASSICAL PIANO
00156644...$14.99

ABOVE ALL
00311024...$12.99

BACH MEETS JAZZ
00198473...$14.99

THE BEATLES
00306412...$16.99

THE BEATLES FOR CLASSICAL PIANO
00312189...$14.99

THE BEATLES – RECITAL SUITES
00275876...$19.99

BEST PIANO SOLOS
00312546...$14.99

BLESSINGS
00156601...$12.99

BLUES CLASSICS
00198656...$12.99

BROADWAY'S BEST
00310669...$14.99

A CELTIC CHRISTMAS
00310629...$12.99

THE CELTIC COLLECTION
00310549...$12.95

CELTIC SONGS WITH A CLASSICAL FLAIR
00280571...$12.99

CHRISTMAS MEDLEYS
00311414...$12.99

CHRISTMAS AT THE MOVIES
00312190...$14.99

CHRISTMAS SONGS FOR CLASSICAL PIANO
00233788...$12.99

CINEMA CLASSICS
00310607...$14.99

CLASSICAL JAZZ
00311083...$12.95

COLDPLAY FOR CLASSICAL PIANO
00137779...$15.99

DISNEY RECITAL SUITES
00249097...$16.99

DISNEY SONGS FOR CLASSICAL PIANO
00311754...$16.99

DISNEY SONGS FOR RAGTIME PIANO
00241379...$16.99

THE FILM SCORE COLLECTION
00311811...$14.99

FOLKSONGS WITH A CLASSICAL FLAIR
00269408...$12.99

GOLDEN SCORES
00233789...$14.99

GOSPEL GREATS
00144351...$12.99

GREAT STANDARDS
00311157...$12.95

THE HYMN COLLECTION
00311071...$12.99

HYMN MEDLEYS
00311349...$12.99

HYMNS IN A CELTIC STYLE
00280705...$12.99

HYMNS WITH A CLASSICAL FLAIR
00269407...$12.99

HYMNS WITH A TOUCH OF JAZZ
00311249...$12.99

JINGLE JAZZ
00310762...$14.99

BILLY JOEL FOR CLASSICAL PIANO
00175310...$15.99

ELTON JOHN FOR CLASSICAL PIANO
00126449...$15.99

LET FREEDOM RING!
00310839...$12.99

ANDREW LLOYD WEBBER
00313227...$15.99

MANCINI MAGIC
00313523...$14.99

MORE DISNEY SONGS FOR CLASSICAL PIANO
00312113...$15.99

MOTOWN HITS
00311295...$12.95

PIAZZOLLA TANGOS
00306870...$15.99

QUEEN FOR CLASSICAL PIANO
00156645...$15.99

RICHARD RODGERS CLASSICS
00310755...$15.99

SHOUT TO THE LORD!
00310699...$14.99

SONGS FROM CHILDHOOD FOR EASY CLASSICAL PIANO
00233688...$12.99

THE SOUND OF MUSIC
00119403...$14.99

SYMPHONIC HYMNS FOR PIANO
00224738...$14.99

TIN PAN ALLEY
00279673...$12.99

TREASURED HYMNS FOR CLASSICAL PIANO
00312112...$14.99

THE TWELVE KEYS OF CHRISTMAS
00144926...$12.99

YULETIDE JAZZ
00311911...$17.99

EASY PIANO

AFRICAN-AMERICAN SPIRITUALS
00310610...$10.99

CATCHY SONGS FOR PIANO
00218387...$12.99

CELTIC DREAMS
00310973...$10.95

CHRISTMAS CAROLS FOR EASY CLASSICAL PIANO
00233686...$12.99

CHRISTMAS POPS
00311126...$14.99

CLASSIC POP/ROCK HITS
00311548...$12.95

A CLASSICAL CHRISTMAS
00310769...$10.95

CLASSICAL MOVIE THEMES
00310975...$12.99

CONTEMPORARY WORSHIP FAVORITES
00311805...$14.99

DISNEY SONGS FOR EASY CLASSICAL PIANO
00144352...$12.99

EARLY ROCK 'N' ROLL
00311093...$12.99

GEORGE GERSHWIN CLASSICS
00110374...$12.99

GOSPEL TREASURES
00310805...$12.99

THE VINCE GUARALDI COLLECTION
00306821...$16.99

HYMNS FOR EASY CLASSICAL PIANO
00160294...$12.99

IMMORTAL HYMNS
00310798...$12.99

JAZZ STANDARDS
00311294...$12.99

LOVE SONGS
00310744...$12.99

THE MOST BEAUTIFUL SONGS FOR EASY CLASSICAL PIANO
00233740...$12.99

POP STANDARDS FOR EASY CLASSICAL PIANO
00233739...$12.99

RAGTIME CLASSICS
00311293...$10.95

SONGS FROM CHILDHOOD FOR EASY CLASSICAL PIANO
00233688...$12.99

SONGS OF INSPIRATION
00103258...$12.99

TIMELESS PRAISE
00310712...$12.95

10,000 REASONS
00126450...$14.99

TV THEMES
00311086...$12.99

21 GREAT CLASSICS
00310717...$12.99

WEEKLY WORSHIP
00145342...$16.99

BIG-NOTE PIANO

CHILDREN'S FAVORITE MOVIE SONGS
00310838...$12.99

CHRISTMAS MUSIC
00311247...$10.95

CLASSICAL FAVORITES
00277368...$12.99

CONTEMPORARY HITS
00310907...$12.99

DISNEY FAVORITES
00277370...$14.99

JOY TO THE WORLD
00310888...$10.95

THE NUTCRACKER
00310908...$10.99

STAR WARS
00277371...$16.99

BEGINNING PIANO SOLOS

AWESOME GOD
00311202...$12.99

CHRISTIAN CHILDREN'S FAVORITES
00310837...$12.99

CHRISTMAS FAVORITES
00311246...$10.95

CHRISTMAS TIME IS HERE
00311334...$12.99

CHRISTMAS TRADITIONS
00311117...$10.99

EASY HYMNS
00311250...$12.99

EVERLASTING GOD
00102710...$10.99

JAZZY TUNES
00311403...$10.95

PIANO DUET

CLASSICAL THEME DUETS
00311350...$10.99

HYMN DUETS
00311544...$12.99

PRAISE & WORSHIP DUETS
00311203...$12.99

STAR WARS
00119405...$14.99

WORSHIP SONGS FOR TWO
00253545...$12.99

HAL•LEONARD®

Visit **www.halleonard.com**
for a complete series listing.

Prices, contents, and availability subject to change without notice.

0419
158